A DAD
AFTER GOD'S OWN HEART

SMART WAYS TO MAXIMIZE FAMILY TIME

PAUL LEWIS

DESIGNED BY ROGER HOFFMAN
EDITED BY JULIE CAMPBELL

A DAD AFTER GOD'S OWN HEART

ISBN: 0-87162-666-7
D7552
PRINTED IN MEXICO

$\mathcal{T}$O EVERY FATHER
WHO HAS WHISPERED
SOLEMN PROMISES TO THE INFANT
CRADLED IN HIS ARMS ...

OR DEEPLY REGRETTED
FATHERING OPPORTUNITIES MISSED
AS HE WATCHES HIS TEENAGER
WALK OUT THE DOOR ...

YOU ARE NOT ALONE!
AND IT IS NEVER TOO LATE TO START
DOING WHAT IS RIGHT!

"THE JUST MAN
WALKETH IN HIS INTEGRITY:
HIS CHILDREN ARE BLESSED
AFTER HIM."

PROVERBS 20:7

INTRODUCTION

Dad, let's understand one another right from the start—on this earth there are no perfect fathers. So, this small volume isn't about fathering perfection. Rather, it's about making progress. It's for fathers like you and me who know they want to do better! We are men desirous of being dads after God's own heart.

If your conscience works like mine, it reminds me regularly that having "a good dad" is essential to each of my kids. Plus, during those infrequent but poignant moments of self-review, I am reminded again that an effective fathering career is terribly important to my own sense of contentment, significance and self-worth. An absence of yearning or desire isn't our problem as fathers. Rather it is our physical and emotional absence that we struggle with most. Becoming a father was easy. It's the daily "doing" of fatherhood that leaves us on the ropes.

I think it's tragic that so little of what we experience in our work-a-day world encourages us to hold family and fathering as high priorities. Compliments, promotions and gold watches aren't offered for good work as a dad. Quality fathering often seems most conspicuous when it is missing. But you and I can change that.

How about committing with me to be a better dad? Start today or tomorrow at the latest. And begin by thumbing through these pages until one of the practical suggestions catches your eye. Use it, then look for another tip and apply that one. Keep coming back for more. Before you know it, you will be way down the road to effective fathering.

Actually, you will be acting as a father out of a heart attitude of love, concern and compassion for your children. And that, my friend, is the essence of what will make you a dad after God's own heart!

A fellow fathering pilgrim,

Paul Lewis

P.S. When you've exhausted the ideas in this volume, try the ones published every other month in *Smart DADS*, the fathering newsletter described at the back of this book. And write to me about the ideas you come up with. I always need the help and encouragement!

$\mathcal{I}$MAGINE THAT YOUR FAMILY HAS BEEN GRANTED FIVE MINUTES ON PRIME-TIME TELEVISION TO PRESENT THE MESSAGE OF YOUR CHOICE TO FAMILIES ALL AROUND THE COUNTRY. DISCUSS AND WRITE DOWN THE MOST IMPORTANT THINGS YOU BELIEVE YOU COULD SAY IN THAT AMOUNT OF TIME. THEN HAVE ONE FAMILY MEMBER READ THE STATEMENT ALOUD. BONUS: MAIL YOUR STATEMENT TO THE EDITOR OF YOUR NEWSPAPER WITH AN EXPLANATION OF HOW IT WAS CREATED. THEN WATCH TO SEE IF IT IS PUBLISHED.

$\mathcal{B}$RIEFLY "TRADE" YOUR CHILD WITH A FRIEND

OR NEIGHBOR WHO HAS A SIMILARLY AGED CHILD.

GIVE EACH CHILD A JOB FOR A SET LENGTH OF TIME

AND FOR SIMILAR PAY. THIS IS A GOOD WAY

TO ACQUAINT YOUR CHILD WITH THE DYNAMICS

OF BEING AN "EMPLOYEE"—THE WORTHY ARTS

OF FOLLOWING DIRECTIONS AND EARNING MONEY.

$\mathcal{I}$N A DAD'S WORLD OF ADULT PRESSURES, IT'S EASY

TO FORGET HOW TO ABANDON YOURSELF TO THE

MOMENT—TO TRULY "PLAY!" SO, DAD, TAKE A SHORT

CLASS FROM YOUR "MIDGET GURUS OF PLAY."

WATCH HOW THEY DO IT, THEN JOIN IN

FOR A "LAB SESSION."

$\mathcal{I}$N PSALM 139, GOD REVEALS THE SPECIAL WAYS

HE THINKS ABOUT EACH INDIVIDUAL. DISCUSS THESE

VERSES, THEN HAVE EACH PERSON SHARE TWO

QUALITIES THEY FEEL ARE SPECIAL ABOUT EACH FAMILY

MEMBER. ALLOW FOLLOW-UP QUESTIONS AND

BE PREPARED FOR A MEMORABLE TIME.

$\mathcal{M}$ount a small marker board in your bathroom. It is an unusual, but very effective place to write notes to each other, think of clever graffiti or announce plans for an upcoming weekend event.

_M_OST COMMUNITIES HAVE A VOLUNTEER

ORGANIZATION THAT ARRANGES HOSTS FOR FOREIGN

STUDENTS VISITING FOR A COUPLE OF WEEKS

OR LONGER. VOLUNTEER YOUR HOME EACH YEAR!

IN ADDITION TO BEING A GREAT EXAMPLE

OF COMMUNITY SERVICE, HOSTING A FOREIGN STUDENT

CAN BUILD INTERNATIONAL INTERESTS AND

UNDERSTANDING IN YOUR CHILDREN.

Working together is a foundational principle of family. Each week, schedule ninety minutes during which everyone tackles their assigned household chores. Make it your policy that when someone finishes early, they will simply pitch in to help someone else finish. Afterwards, reward yourselves with a snack together around the table!

$\mathcal{N}$EXT TIME YOU HEAD FOR THE VIDEO STORE,

STOP INSTEAD AT YOUR LOCAL LIBRARY AND PICK UP

AN ENTERTAINING VIDEO THERE. MOST PUBLIC

LIBRARIES RENT A VARIETY OF INTERESTING

TRAVELOGUES AND INSTRUCTIONAL TAPES AS WELL

AS DRAMATIC CLASSICS WELL WORTH WATCHING.

*T*HE "ACTS" APPROACH TO PRAYER IS A USEFUL

WAY TO HELP YOUR FAMILY LEARN THE BASIC

ELEMENTS IN CONVERSING WITH GOD.

"A" STANDS FOR ADORATION (PRAISE);
"C"—CONFESSION;
"T"—THANKSGIVING; AND
"S"—SUPPLICATION (REQUESTS).

BENEFIT: AS EACH PERSON KEEPS THESE FOUR

ELEMENTS IN MIND, THEY WILL LEARN THAT PRAYER

IS FAR MORE THAN JUST ASKING GOD FOR THINGS.

"*H*OME LOANS" CAN TEACH CHILDREN A LOT

ABOUT THE USES AND ABUSES OF CONSUMER CREDIT.

TRY ALLOWING YOUR KIDS TO LEND EACH OTHER

MONEY AT A REASONABLE RATE OF INTEREST. BEFORE

LONG THEY'LL UNDERSTAND CONCEPTS LIKE CREDIT

RISK, CREDIT HISTORY,

INSTALLMENT

PAYMENTS AND WHY

BANKS REQUIRE COLLATERAL.

16

$\mathcal{W}$HEN TENSIONS BUILD BETWEEN YOU AND YOUR CHILD, TAKE THE INITIATIVE AND INVITE THEM TO BREAKFAST OR LUNCH WITH YOU. ALLOW THE FOOD AND NEUTRAL ATMOSPHERE TO HELP OPEN THE LINES OF COMMUNICATION. LISTEN HARD. SPEAK GENTLY. MODEL EFFECTIVE PROBLEM SOLVING AND MATURE ATTITUDES, AND READ PROVERBS 15:1-2 TOGETHER.

$\mathcal{T}$ONIGHT, CHOOSE A SERVICE PROJECT YOUR FAMILY

CAN PERFORM TOGETHER THAT WILL HELP SOMEONE

IN NEED. IDEAS: FIX A MEAL FOR A SICK NEIGHBOR,

TAKE SUPPLIES TO A HOMELESS SHELTER, BABY-SIT

FOR A SINGLE PARENT, VISIT AND READ TO AN ELDERLY

PERSON, ETC.

*K*EEP LEARNING! ASK YOUR CHILD TO TEACH YOU

A SKILL THEY HAVE DEVELOPED OR A CONCEPT THEY

HAVE LEARNED. IT COULD BE AN OUTDOOR SPORT,

A VIDEO GAME, A COMPUTER PROGRAM OR SOMETHING

THEY HAVE JUST STUDIED IN HISTORY, SCIENCE

OR SOCIAL STUDIES AT SCHOOL.

"Mystery favors" make a very special family tradition. Simply draw the name of another family member from a hat and agree that over the next three or seven days you will do a secret favor for the person whose name you drew. Then when you get together again, try to guess the favor done and who may have performed this act of love. This is a game your family will never grow tired of.

*T*ELL YOUR TEENAGERS YOU WILL LET THEM
BEGIN DATING AFTER A CERTAIN BIRTHDAY AND AFTER
THEY HAVE REVIEWED WITH YOU THEIR WRITTEN
DATING PURPOSE STATEMENT. THE STATEMENT SHOULD
INCLUDE A CLEAR EXPRESSION OF THE PURPOSES
FOR DATING, THEIR STANDARDS FOR WHOM THEY
WILL DATE AND THE BEHAVIORS THEY WILL AVOID,
SUCH AS ALCOHOL, DRUGS, LEVELS OF PHYSICAL
AFFECTION, ETC.

Make a list of the vacations and other experiences you would like to enjoy with each of your children before they are grown and gone. Now, list the years you have remaining (God willing) and match activities to dates. If you are fortunate, you will still have enough time to complete them all. If you don't, then make the tough choices and redeem the time!

To grow up secure, children need both love and limits. Check yourself: How many times did you verbally or physically express your love to each child this past week? Should you work at doubling the frequency this coming week?

23

*Y*OUR FIRST THREE MINUTES HOME FROM WORK OR A BUSINESS TRIP, FOLLOWED BY THE NEXT FIFTEEN MINUTES, SET THE TONE FOR THE REST OF THE EVENING. AS YOU ARRIVE HOME, GIVE A FEW QUICK HONKS IN THE DRIVEWAY OR GARAGE TO START THE EXCITEMENT, RING THE DOORBELL SEVERAL TIMES, AND ADD SEVERAL UNEXPECTED SPIN-AROUNDS TO YOUR ORDINARY HUGS. CRUCIAL TIP: DON'T SIT DOWN, PICK UP THE PAPER, THE PHONE OR THE MAIL UNTIL YOU'VE MADE CONTACT INDIVIDUALLY WITH EVERY FAMILY MEMBER.

$\mathcal{W}$HAT DOES YOUR CHILD READ FOR PLEASURE?

CHECK IT OUT. HELP YOUR CHILD AVOID LITERATURE

WITH THE FOLLOWING THEMES: ADOLESCENTS

ARE MORE PERCEPTIVE THAN ADULTS; PARENTAL

EXPERIENCE ISN'T RELEVANT TO TODAY'S WORLD;

PERSONALITY AND APPEARANCE CAN BE EASILY

TRANSFORMED; AND SEX IS THE MOST

IMPORTANT INTERACTION BETWEEN

A MAN AND A WOMAN.

$\mathcal{W}$ASHING CARS AND WINDOWS IS MORE "DANGEROUS" FOR DADS AND A LOT MORE FUN FOR KIDS IF YOU PUT THE CLEANING SOLUTION IN A SQUIRT GUN. TRY A BIG, SOFT PAINT BRUSH AND BUCKET OF SOAPY WATER, SO YOUR CHILD CAN HELP BY "PAINTING" THE DIRT OFF THE CAR.

$\mathcal{K}$EEP A LIST IN YOUR PERSONAL PLANNER TITLED

"FAMILY ACTIVITIES." ADD IDEAS AS YOU READ

IN THE CALENDAR SECTION OF YOUR LOCAL PAPER,

TALK WITH FRIENDS, AND OBSERVE OTHER FAMILIES.

LOG THE PHONE NUMBERS OF LOCAL MUSEUMS,

LIBRARIES OR THE NEWSPAPER'S CITY DESK TO CALL

FOR UPDATES AND DETAILS.

*A*GREE WITH YOUR FAVORITE GOLFING PARTNER TO BRING YOUR TEENAGERS ALONG FOR YOUR NEXT ROUND. EACH FATHER/CHILD PAIR USES ONE BALL AND ALTERNATES SHOTS AS THEY COMPETE AGAINST THE OTHER PAIR. WORKS WITH MINIATURE GOLF AND YOUNGER KIDS, TOO!

*J*UMP-START COMMUNICATION BY ASKING YOUR CHILD

TO COMPLETE A SENTENCE LIKE: "THE MOST FUN

I HAD THIS WEEK WAS ..." "I'M MOST SCARED WHEN

YOU AND MOM ..." "I COULD GET ALONG WITHOUT

MANY OF MY FRIENDS EXCEPT FOR..." "THE DUMBEST

THING I'VE EVER SEEN A PARENT DO IS ...."

MAKE UP SOME OF YOUR OWN, TOO.

$\mathcal{F}$OR THE NEXT SEVEN DAYS IN A ROW,

MAKE "I LOVE YOU" THE FIRST AND LAST WORDS

YOU SAY EACH DAY TO YOUR WIFE AND CHILDREN.

*K*IDS LOVE MAIL. SO MAIL YOUR CHILD A NOTE
FROM THE OFFICE ON COMPANY STATIONERY.
EXPRESS YOUR APPRECIATION FOR ONE OF THEIR BEST
CHARACTER STRENGTHS AND THE CONTRIBUTION
THEY MAKE TO YOUR FAMILY. ENCLOSE A STICK
OF GUM OR SOMETHING FROM THE RECEPTIONIST'S
CANDY JAR.

ON YOUR NEXT WEDDING ANNIVERSARY,

ASK YOUR WIFE TO SLIP OFF HER WEDDING RING

FOR A MOMENT. THEN IN FRONT OF THE KIDS, RECITE

TO HER YOUR WEDDING VOWS AS YOU REPLACE IT

ON HER FINGER. MORE THAN HOW MUCH YOU LOVE

THEM, YOUR CHILDREN FIND THEIR SECURITY

IN KNOWING HOW MUCH YOU LOVE THEIR MOM.

*A*FTER AN ESPECIALLY TOUGH DAY AT WORK,

AND BEFORE YOU HEAD HOME (OR AT SOME STOPPING

POINT ALONG THE WAY), TAKE TEN MINUTES TO CLOSE

YOUR EYES AND CONSCIOUSLY UNWIND. THE KIDS WILL

BE ANXIOUS TO SEE YOU, AND YOU WILL BE BETTER

PREPARED TO ENJOY THEIR ATTENTION AND LISTEN

TO THEM RECOUNT THE DAY'S EVENTS IF YOU'RE NOT

TRYING TO RELAX AT THE SAME TIME.

*I*N A MODERN LANGUAGE TRANSLATION, READ WITH

YOUR TEENAGER THROUGH THE BOOK OF PROVERBS

IN THE OLD TESTAMENT (ALTERNATE EVERY FIVE

VERSES). STOP AND COMMENT ON THE TRUTHS YOU

DEEPLY BELIEVE, HAVE EXPERIENCED YOURSELF

OR HAVE WATCHED A FRIEND EXPERIENCE.

34

$\mathcal{I}$F YOU'RE A LONG-DISTANCE DAD, KEEP A 3" X 5"

CARD HANDY TO LIST THOUGHTS AND QUESTIONS

YOU WANT TO INCORPORATE INTO YOUR NEXT CALL

TO YOUR CHILD. THAT WAY, YOU'LL NEVER BE STUCK

FOR SOMETHING PURPOSEFUL TO TALK ABOUT.

*A*LWAYS BE SPECIFIC WHEN YOU PRAISE YOUR CHILD OR YOUR WIFE. INSTEAD OF SAYING, "YOU DID A NICE JOB ON THE YARD," SAY, "YOU SHAPED THE HEDGES JUST RIGHT, AND THE FLOWER BEDS LOOK GREAT SINCE YOU RAKED AND WEEDED THEM."

$\mathcal{N}$EVER DEBATE IN FRONT OF YOUNGER CHILDREN

ABOUT A JUDGMENT CALL YOUR WIFE HAS MADE.

RATHER, DISCUSS IT PRIVATELY. AS THEY GROW OLDER,

ALLOWING CHILDREN TO OBSERVE YOUR RESPECT

FOR EACH OTHER WHILE HANDLING A DISAGREEMENT

CAN HELP THEM MATURE IN THIS IMPORTANT AREA.

Surprise your child (especially a teenager) with breakfast in bed. The love and servanthood you express with such an act can diffuse tensions and encourage some excellent moments of sharing and conversation. Works wonders with wives, too!

$\mathcal{T}$HOSE PET NAMES YOU CALL YOUR CHILD MAKE

AN IMPORTANT CONTRIBUTION TO HIS OR HER

DEVELOPING SELF-CONCEPT. BE SURE THE NAMES

REFLECT AND REINFORCE POSITIVE PHYSICAL AND

CHARACTER QUALITIES.

$\mathcal{A}$ CHILD IS MOST ATTENTIVE WHEN LOOKED

STRAIGHT IN THE EYE. EYE CONTACT IS A PRIMARY

MEANS OF CONVEYING LOVE, ESPECIALLY WHEN YOUR

GAZE IS ACCOMPANIED BY A SMILE AND KIND WORDS.

TIP: NEVER USE AN AVOIDANCE OF EYE CONTACT

AS PUNISHMENT, OR USE EYE CONTACT ONLY WHEN

GIVING INSTRUCTIONS, A REPRIMAND OR CRITICISM.

$\mathscr{P}$RAISE YOUR CHILD BY CREATING A PERSONAL

ACROSTIC. PRINT THE LETTERS OF THEIR FIRST NAME

DOWN THE LEFT SIDE OF YOUR PAPER AND LIST

A CHARACTER STRENGTH THEY POSSESS THAT BEGINS

WITH EACH LETTER. THEN DESIGN A SPECIAL MOMENT

TO PRESENT THE ACROSTIC IN A LETTER OR A SIMPLE

FRAME. TALK ABOUT THE REASON YOU SELECTED

EACH QUALITY.

$\mathcal{E}$NCOURAGE GROWTH IN A FRIEND'S MARRIAGE

BY VOLUNTEERING TO BABY-SIT THEIR CHILDREN ONE

NIGHT A MONTH FOR THE NEXT THREE MONTHS.

THIS WILL GUARANTEE THEM THREE SPECIAL "DATES"

IN A ROW. AND NO DOUBT THE FAVOR WILL

BE RETURNED.

$\mathcal{W}$HAT ARE YOU FAMOUS FOR IN YOUR FAMILY?

ASK EVERYONE TONIGHT AT DINNER. IF YOU'RE NOT

HAPPY WITH THE ANSWERS, INITIATE SOME NEW

TRADITIONS—A SPECIAL MEAL YOU COOK, STORY YOU

TELL, ACTIVITY YOU REPEAT WITH EACH CHILD, ETC.

THE LEGACY YOU WILL LEAVE BEHIND IS YOUR CHOICE!

*W*ORD STUDIES IN SCRIPTURE CAN BE FUN AND CAN QUICKLY HELP YOUR CHILDREN LEARN TO SEARCH GOD'S WORD FOR THEMSELVES. USING A SIMPLE CONCORDANCE OR COMPUTER BIBLE SOFTWARE PROGRAM, MAKE A LIST OF VERSES ON THEMES LIKE "JOY," "LIFE," "PEACE," "HEAVEN," "ANGELS," "OBEY," ETC.

STAGE A FAMILY CONTEST TO SEE WHO HAS THE

LARGEST SMILE. MEASURE EACH PERSON'S SMILE WITH

A TAPE MEASURE (IF YOU CAN GET THEM

TO STOP LAUGHING LONG ENOUGH). GIVE A PACK

OF SUGARLESS GUM AS A PRIZE TO THE WINNER.

READ TOGETHER PROVERBS 15:13 FOR THE

SCRIPTURAL APPLICATION.

$\mathcal{T}$AKE A TIP FROM THE OLD FARM COUPLE WHO SENT

TLC (TENDER LOVING CARE) SIGNALS TO EACH OTHER

WHEN EXTRA ENCOURAGEMENT WAS NEEDED. IF THE

HUSBAND NEEDED SOME TLC, HE'D WALK INTO THE

KITCHEN AND THROW HIS HAT DOWN ON THE TABLE.

THIS SIGNALED HIS WIFE THAT SHE NEEDED

TO ENCOURAGE HIM. SIMILARLY, IF HE DISCOVERED

THAT SHE WAS WEARING HER APRON BACKWARDS,

IT WAS A SIGN THAT SHE NEEDED HELP TO BEAR HER

BURDENS. WHAT COULD YOUR TLC SIGNALS BE?

*T*ONIGHT AT DINNER, MAKE A RULE. BEFORE EACH

FAMILY MEMBER CAN START EATING, HE OR SHE MUST

SHARE ONE NEW THING LEARNED TODAY. (AND IF ONE

CAN'T BE THOUGHT OF, THAT PERSON MAY BE EXCUSED

TO LOOK IN THE DICTIONARY FOR A NEW WORD

TO SHARE.)

ON YOUR BUSINESS CARD, UNDER YOUR OCCUPATION,

CONSIDER ADDING "FATHER OF ..." AND LISTING THE

NAMES OF YOUR CHILDREN. IMAGINE HOW YOUR KIDS

WILL FEEL WHEN THEY GET EQUAL BILLING

WITH YOUR CAREER.

SOMETIME EACH WEEKEND, LEAD A TWENTY-MINUTE

REVIEW OF YOUR FAMILY SCHEDULES FOR THE COMING

WEEK. IT IS AN OPPORTUNITY NOT ONLY TO SORT OUT

THE LOGISTICS AND CONFLICTS, BUT ALSO

TO STRENGTHEN YOUR FAMILY BY BEING THERE

FOR EACH OTHER AT IMPORTANT EVENTS.

*G*RACE AT MEALS CAN EASILY LAPSE INTO A RATHER LIFELESS ROUTINE. TRY ENLIVENING THESE IMPORTANT PRAYERS BY ADDING SOME VARIETY:

- SLOW DOWN THE PRAYER SO THAT EACH THOUGHT IS EMPHASIZED.

- DISCUSS THE PRAYER'S KEY IDEAS IN THE FIRST FEW MOMENTS OF THE MEAL.

- PRAY AT THE END OF THE MEAL.

- HAVE EACH FAMILY MEMBER OFFER A SHORT PORTION OF THE PRAYER.

- START EATING WITHOUT A PRAYER AND WHEN SOMEONE NOTICES, LEAD A DISCUSSION ABOUT WHY PRAYER IS IMPORTANT. TALK ABOUT WHAT SHOULD BE INCLUDED IN THE PRAYER. HOW SPECIFIC SHOULD IT BE? WHAT CAUSES PRAYER TO LOSE ITS SIGNIFICANCE?

"SWITCHEROO" HAS ALWAYS BEEN A FUN FAMILY

GAME AT OUR HOUSE, NO MATTER WHAT THE AGES

OF THE CHILDREN. NEXT DINNERTIME, EVERYONE

SIMPLY SWITCHES CHAIRS AT THE TABLE AND TRIES

TO ACT AND TALK LIKE THE PERSON WHO USUALLY

SITS IN THAT CHAIR. THE LAUGHTER AND INSIGHTS

ARE ALWAYS IMMENSE!

$\mathcal{F}$IVE MINUTE "LOVE NOTES" ARE A SUPERB WAY
TO ENCOURAGE A RELATIVE OR FRIEND WHO MAY
BE FACING SURGERY OR ANOTHER DIFFICULT MOMENT.
GATHER THE FAMILY AROUND A TABLE FOR FIVE
MINUTES, GIVE EACH A BLANK SHEET OF PAPER AND
SOME CRAYONS OR MARKERS. THEN ASK EACH PERSON
TO DRAW SOME SORT OF DECORATIVE BORDER ON
THEIR PAGE. NEXT ASK THEM TO WRITE A SENTENCE
IN THE MIDDLE WHICH DESCRIBES A QUALITY THEY
APPRECIATE IN THE RELATIVE OR PERSON YOU HAVE
IN MIND. (TAKE DICTATION FROM A CHILD WHO CAN'T
WRITE YET.) ANOTHER IDEA IS FOR EACH PERSON
TO WRITE A FAVORITE SCRIPTURE VERSE
OF ENCOURAGEMENT INSIDE THE BORDER. WHEN YOU
ARE FINISHED, SIMPLY FOLD THE SHEETS INTO AN
ENVELOPE. A POSITIVE RESPONSE FROM THE PERSON
YOU MAIL THIS TO IS GUARANTEED!

The dad who says, "I won't even discuss it" is not showing strength, but is actually revealing weakness. The strong father is able to withstand the rigors of negotiation because he is committed to a relationship with his children and is willing to put in the time and effort to achieve it.

$\mathcal{L}$ IST THE FRUITS OF THE SPIRIT FROM GALATIANS

5:22-23 DOWN THE LEFT SIDE OF A SMALL POSTER.

ACROSS THE TOP WRITE THE NAMES OF EACH FAMILY

MEMBER. HANG THE POSTER ON THE REFRIGERATOR

DOOR. THEN AT DINNER TIME PASS THE SHEET

AROUND AND ASK FAMILY MEMBERS TO COMMENT

ON AND ADD A TALLY MARK NEXT TO THE SPIRITUAL

FRUITS THEY HAVE SEEN THE OTHERS EXPRESS OVER

THE PAST COUPLE OF DAYS OR WEEKS.

$\mathcal{D}$O YOUR KIDS KNOW THAT THEY ARE AT LEAST

AS IMPORTANT AS EVERYONE ELSE WITH WHOM YOU

MAKE APPOINTMENTS IN YOUR DAILY PLANNER?

TAKE YOUR APPOINTMENT BOOK TO DINNER TONIGHT

AND SCHEDULE A SPECIAL TIME WITH EACH MEMBER

IN YOUR FAMILY OVER THE NEXT WEEK OR TWO.

THEN TURN A FEW PAGES AND BOOK A SECOND

APPOINTMENT.

$\mathcal{A}$ "COVENANT PLACE" FOR FAMILY PRAYERS

IS A VERY SUCCESSFUL STRATEGY IN MANY HOMES.

SELECT A SPECIAL SPOT CONDUCIVE TO GROUP

PRAYER, BIBLE READING AND WORSHIP. STUDIES

SHOW THAT A CONSISTENT LOCATION BUILDS

CONTINUITY AND A SENSE OF FAMILIAR TRADITION.

(FOR FRESHNESS: MOVE TO AN ALTERNATE PLACE

EVERY FIFTH OR SIXTH TIME.)

*A*RE YOU OVERDUE IN EXPRESSING GRATITUDE
TO YOUR CHILDREN FOR THE LITTLE THINGS THEY DO?
TRY COMPLIMENTING THEM ON THEIR:

- CHEERFUL DISPOSITION
- WILLINGNESS TO HELP AROUND THE HOUSE
- THOUGHTFULNESS OF OTHERS
- KEEPING A NEAT ROOM
- DRIVING THE CAR WELL
- CALLING HOME WHEN LATE
- USING MONEY WISELY
- CARING FOR CLOTHES
- KEEPING TOYS PICKED UP
- HELPING MOM

AND HOW ABOUT THE THANKS YOUR WIFE IS DUE FOR:

- HER LOVE AND COMPANIONSHIP
- SMILING EVEN WHEN SHE'S TIRED
- KEEPING HERSELF BEAUTIFUL FOR YOU
- THE DOMESTIC CHORES SHE TIRELESSLY
  COMPLETES

$\mathcal{P}$UT A TINY STICKER OR PEN MARK ON YOUR

WRISTWATCH FACE TO REMIND YOU OF A CHALLENGING

MOMENT YOUR CHILD WILL FACE DURING THE DAY.

THEY'LL NEED YOUR BEST THOUGHTS AND PRAYERS.

58

When you want a child to carefully consider a particular situation or decision, ask him to write down a pros and cons list, or all the reasons he should be allowed to do or have something. Then talk it over. Reinforce the principle that when all the facts are in, the right decision usually becomes obvious.

$\mathcal{F}$ROM TIME TO TIME, BRING TO THE DINNER TABLE THE "DEAR ABBY" ADVICE COLUMN FROM YOUR LOCAL PAPER. READ THE QUESTION, AND BEFORE READING THE COLUMNIST'S ANSWER, DISCUSS WHAT ADVICE EACH OF YOU WOULD GIVE. THEN TAKE IT A STEP FURTHER AND SAY WHAT ADVICE YOU BELIEVE GOD WOULD GIVE. TIE YOUR ANSWER TO A SPECIFIC SCRIPTURE OR BIBLICAL EXAMPLE EVERY TIME POSSIBLE.

A SMART DAD IS NEVER AT A LOSS FOR GOOD

CONVERSATION WITH HIS TEENAGER. HE STAYS

IN TOUCH BY READING PORTIONS OF EACH OF HIS

CHILD'S HIGH SCHOOL TEXTBOOKS.

*I*N A DISCUSSION ABOUT FATHERING, NOTED

AUTHOR, PASTOR AND TEACHER DR. CHARLES

SWINDOLL COMMENTED ON WHAT HE WOULD DO

DIFFERENTLY AS A FATHER IF HE COULD DO IT OVER

AGAIN. HIS FIRST RESPONSE WAS SIMPLE AND WORTH

TAKING TO HEART: "I WOULD SAY 'YES' MORE OFTEN!"

$\mathcal{T}$AKE A "VACATION" FROM TELEVISION FOR A

WEEK AND SEE WHAT HAPPENS. SET OUT SOME

LONG-FORGOTTEN TABLE GAMES, CRAFT MATERIALS,

FAMILY PHOTO ALBUMS AND FAVORITE STORY BOOKS

WHERE THEY'LL BE EASILY SPOTTED.

*T*HE ATMOSPHERE IN YOUR HOME IS MORE THE RESULT OF THE WORDS SPOKEN THAN THE FURNISHINGS. DOES YOUR FAMILY HEAR LOVING WORDS OR STRIFE-FILLED WORDS, CONSIDERATE WORDS OR SELFISH WORDS, COMPLIMENTARY WORDS OR DEMEANING WORDS, QUIET WORDS OR HARSH WORDS? ASK EACH FAMILY MEMBER TO LIST THE WORDS THEY FEEL ARE MOST OFTEN HEARD IN YOUR HOME. COMPARE LISTS AND TALK ABOUT THE RESULTS. THEN READ JAMES 3 TOGETHER.

Every dad has his "specialties"—skills and knowledge he possesses in greater measure than others. What are your specialties? Have you passed them on to your children? Have they arrived at the right age to learn another one? When I ask a man about a unique skill he has learned, there's always a special sparkle in his response when he can say, "My dad taught me!"

*C*ONSIDERING HOW IMPORTANT HAVING A FATHER AND
GRANDFATHER ARE TO CHILDREN AND GRANDCHILDREN,
ARE YOU TAKING CARE OF YOURSELF? ARE YOU EATING
RIGHT? EXERCISING? AVOIDING RISKY HEALTH HABITS?
SET A PHYSICAL FITNESS GOAL FOR YOURSELF TODAY.

$\mathscr{R}$EMINISCE WITH YOUR CHILD OR AS A FAMILY

ABOUT SOME GREAT TIMES YOU'VE SHARED. THEN

SELECT THE TOP FIVE AND REPEAT THEM

AS SOON AS POSSIBLE.

*I*F YOUR COMPANY WERE MANAGED WITH THE VERY

SAME AMOUNT OF FORETHOUGHT, GOAL SETTING

AND PLANNING THAT YOU ROUTINELY GIVE TO YOUR

MARRIAGE AND FAMILY RELATIONSHIPS, WOULD YOU

STILL BE IN BUSINESS IN SIX MONTHS? FOR MOST

OF US, THE APPLICATION WITHIN OUR FAMILIES

OF JUST FIVE PERCENT OF THE MANAGEMENT SKILLS WE

USE IN THE WORKPLACE WOULD PROBABLY

REVOLUTIONIZE OUR RELATIONSHIPS.

"GUESS WHAT?" MAKES AN EXCELLENT TABLE

OR "DRIVE TIME" CONVERSATION STARTER

FOR DISCOVERING WHAT HAS HAPPENED THAT DAY

TO OTHER FAMILY MEMBERS. IN ROTATION, ASK

"GUESS WHAT HAPPENED TO ME TODAY?" OR, "GUESS

WHO I SAW?" "GUESS WHAT I LEARNED?" OR SOME

OTHER "GUESS WHAT"-TYPE OF QUESTION.

"WHEN I SAW THIS I THOUGHT OF YOU!"

ARE MAGIC WORDS WHEN SCRAWLED ON A NOTE

ATTACHED TO AN OBJECT LEFT OUT FOR YOUR WIFE OR

CHILD TO DISCOVER. THE ITEM COULD BE A FLOWER,

PICTURE OR CLIPPING FROM A NEWSPAPER

OR MAGAZINE, COSTUME JEWELRY, TRAVEL BROCHURE

OR PIECE OF THEIR FAVORITE CANDY. IT'S ALWAYS

THE LITTLE THOUGHTS THAT COUNT BIG.

CHALLENGE YOUR KIDS TO LIST TWENTY THINGS THAT WERE NOT YET INVENTED WHEN YOU WERE THEIR AGE (COMPUTERS, WATERBEDS, CALL WAITING, TRASH COMPACTORS, INLINE SKATES, ETC.). ASK WHICH ONES ARE THE MOST HELPFUL AND WHICH WE WOULD BE BETTER OFF WITHOUT. CAP THE CONVERSATION WITH A PRAYER OF THANKSGIVING FOR ALL THE GOOD THINGS YOU ENJOY AS A FAMILY IN TODAY'S WORLD.

$\mathcal{H}$OW OFTEN DO YOU SERVE YOUR FAMILY

BY COOKING A FAMILY MEAL? ONCE A WEEK? MONTH?

YEAR? MOST OF THE WORLD'S GREAT CHEFS ARE MEN.

SO WHY NOT ASSIGN YOURSELF ONE MEAL A MONTH

OR WEEK AND CULTIVATE YOUR CULINARY ARTISTRY?

EVERYONE HAS TO START SOMEWHERE ... AND THINK

HOW IMPRESSED AND AMAZED YOUR WIFE AND KIDS

WILL BE!

A CRITICAL SPIRIT CAN PARALYZE FAMILY RELATIONSHIPS. READ TOGETHER JESUS' WORDS ABOUT CRITICISM IN MATTHEW 7:1-5. RECALL LUIS NIZER'S OBSERVATION: WHEN YOU POINT YOUR FINGER AT SOMEONE ELSE, YOU HAVE THREE POINTED AT YOURSELF. DISCUSS HOW CRITICISM IS TYPICALLY GIVEN AND RECEIVED IN YOUR FAMILY. IS IT BALANCED WITH PRAISE?

$\mathcal{H}$OW LONG HAS IT BEEN SINCE YOU'VE WRITTEN A SIMPLE AND SINCERE THANK YOU NOTE TO A SCHOOL TEACHER FOR THEIR EFFORTS ON BEHALF OF YOUR CHILD? HOW ABOUT TO A COACH, SUNDAY SCHOOL TEACHER, BOSS, NEIGHBOR OR EXTENDED FAMILY MEMBER? IT TAKES LESS THAN FIVE MINUTES TO PEN THREE OR FOUR SENTENCES.

*A*sk your kids which Bible family they would have liked to live in and why. How would they have related to other family members? How did God use these families to accomplish or illustrate his purposes? Insight: You can learn much about your children's feelings and attitudes toward their own family by the answers they give.

$\mathcal{W}$ITH A PEN IN HAND, ANSWER ON PAPER

THE QUESTION: "WHAT ONE SIMPLE CHANGE COULD

YOU IMPLEMENT THAT WOULD GREATLY IMPROVE YOUR

CHANCES OF BECOMING A BETTER FATHER

OR HUSBAND THREE MONTHS FROM NOW?"

*O*N YOUR NEXT FAMILY TRIP TO CHURCH,

A RESTAURANT OR THE STORE, LEAVE TEN MINUTES

EARLY AND PARK THREE OR FOUR BLOCKS AWAY

FROM YOUR DESTINATION. THE WALK WILL GIVE YOU

SOME EXTRA EXERCISE AND A FEW MINUTES

OF UNHURRIED CONVERSATION

ABOUT YOUR DAY OR WHAT YOU

MAY SEE ALONG THE WAY.

$\mathcal{A}$CCORDING TO PSYCHOLOGICAL RESEARCH, ONE'S LAST CONSCIOUS THOUGHTS TEND TO STAY ACTIVE IN THE SUBCONSCIOUS ALL NIGHT. TAKE ADVANTAGE OF THIS PRINCIPLE BY MAKING SURE THAT YOUR CHILDREN END THEIR DAY ON A POSITIVE NOTE RATHER THAN A STERNLY REPEATED: "GO TO SLEEP!" TRY REVIEWING OR REPEATING A SCRIPTURE VERSE, SINGING A SHORT SONG OR PROVIDING FEEDBACK ON A CHARACTER STRENGTH YOU SEE DEVELOPING IN THEM.

The fathering tips and ideas in this book first appeared in Smart DADS newsletter.

☐ YES! Please enter my subscription to Smart DADS newsletter. I understand that a "Dad Talk" cassette will arrive with each third, bi-monthly issue and that, should I become dissatisfied, the unfulfilled portion of my subscription will be cheerfully refunded.

☐ Send me a year of *Smart Dads* (6 issues and 2 tapes) at the special introductory rate of $18.50.
That's 23% off the regular price!

☐ This is a gift subscription. My name and address are attached. Please send a gift card signed:

_____

Name _____

Address _____

City/State/Zip _____

Phone: (____)_____

Payment method (check one):
☐ Check enclosed
☐ Please charge my ☐ VISA ☐ MasterCard

No. ____ - ____ - ____

Expires_____ Signature: _____

Mail this coupon to:
SMART DADS
Family University
P.O. Box 500050
San Diego, CA 92150-0050